Lin

P9-CBP-012

SCHOLASTIC

OVERHEAD WRITING LESSONS

POWERFUL PARAGRAPHS

by Carol Rawlings Miller
and Sarah Glasscock

NEW YORK • TORONTO • LONDON • AUCKLAND • SYDNEY

MEXICO CITY • NEW DELHI • HONG KONG • BUENOS AIRES

Teaching *Resources*

This book is dedicated to Jack.

—CRM

Acknowledgments

Sincerest thanks are due to Jeanne and
Milton Miller and Charles and Joan Rawlings,
for being devoted, babysitting grandparents,
and to my husband James Miller, for patience.

More than one editor made this series possible.
I really am indebted to Ellen Ungaro—not only
for her expertise and encouragement, but
for her sense of humor. I also wish to thank
Virginia Dooley; she has been, amongst other
things, patient. And to Wendy Murray, for
weighing in helpfully, many thanks.

—CRM

The overheads and reproducible pages in this book may be reproduced for classroom use.
No other part of the publication may be reproduced in whole or in part, or stored in a retrieval system,
or transmitted in any forms or by any means, electronic, mechanical, photocopying, recording,
or otherwise, without written permission of the publisher. For information regarding permissions,
write to Scholastic Inc., 557 Broadway, New York, NY 10012.

Cover Design by Josué Castilleja
Cover Illustration by Eric Brace
Interior Design by Brian LaRossa

Book ISBN 0-439-56817-X
Product ISBN 0-439-23193-0
Copyright © 2005 by Carol Rawlings Miller and Sarah Glasscock
All rights reserved.
Printed in the U.S.A.

4 5 6 7 8 9 10   40   12 11 10 09 08 07 06

Contents

Introduction

Learning to paragraph is an essential stage for all writers. The ability to organize and sustain a coherent composition derives from paragraphing competence. The activities and exercises in this book will help students develop strong paragraphing skills by having them read, analyze, and write paragraphs.

▲ The Approach of This Book

This book addresses the following aspects of paragraphing:

- the definition of a paragraph
- the types of paragraphs
- a paragraph's structure
- developing a paragraph
- transition words in a paragraph
- editing and proofreading paragraphs

We suggest that you teach the lessons in sequence, as they build upon one another. Many of the paragraphs in the lessons on the structure and development of paragraphs are expository since students will encounter this type most frequently.

An overhead transparency accompanies each of the ten lessons in this book. The transparencies are designed to give a brief overview and to present examples for the class to analyze together. Each lesson also includes at least one reproducible that provides students with more practice and/or reference sheets. We suggest that you display the overhead for reference as students work on the reproducibles.

The teaching pages display the pertinent National Language Arts Standards for each lesson. You'll also find information here about how to present the overhead transparencies and the reproducibles. Writing Practice is a feature that allows students to apply the skills in their own writing. Some lessons include a section called Enriching the Lesson, which expounds on the topic.

▲ On Teaching Paragraphing

When you ask students to write, remind them to paragraph and indent. Keep in mind, however, that an overemphasis on paragraphing can lead beginning writers to become prematurely attentive to structure at a time when they need to build stamina as writers.

Also keep in mind that there are so many skills involved in writing, and we teachers don't want to overwhelm and discourage students. If a child writes his or her first amazing story but forgets to indent some paragraphs, it's more important to celebrate what is happening rather than what is not. The lack of indentations can be fixed easily, while the lack of a coherent narrative cannot. It's also extremely important to emphasize that producing a polished piece of writing is a process. Clear and coherent writing takes more than one draft. All kinds of problems can be fixed in the later drafts of a work.

▲ On Overhead Writing Lessons

Strong Sentences, *Powerful Paragraphs*, and *Exceptional Essays* comprise the Overhead Writing Lessons series of books. Each book targets and teaches specific grammar and writing skills that will make your students better and more confident writers.

Powerful Paragraphs

National Language Arts Standards:

▲ Recognizes a paragraph as a group of sentences about one main idea

▲ Uses paragraph form in writing

Overhead Transparency

◆ Powerful Paragraphs

Reproducibles

◆ Different Types of Paragraphs

◆ What Am I?

◆ Order! Order!

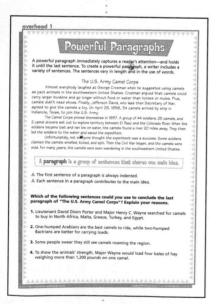

◆ Purpose ◆

To introduce the concept of a powerful paragraph

Without subdivisions or clear markers of organization, writing becomes confusing and tiring to read. Students often have a tendency to ramble on about a topic, and they forget to indent. Learning how to write powerful paragraphs will help students organize their thoughts more effectively. Their ideas will flow more logically and smoothly.

▲ **Launching Activity: Powerful Paragraphs (Overhead 1)**

After going over the introductory sentence on the overhead and the information about paragraphs, examine "The U.S. Army Camel Corps" passage with students. Point out the indentations for each paragraph.

To ease students into the exercise at the bottom of the overhead, you may want to model your response to the first sentence. *The first sentence tells about where the Army looked for camels to bring to the United States. That information would fit in the first paragraph because that paragraph is about how the Army decided to use camels and when they arrived in this country. The last paragraph is about when and why the Army decided not to use the camels anymore.* By doing this, you'll be indirectly guiding students to think about the main idea of each paragraph. Also call on different students to read aloud the last paragraph with one of the four sentences attached to the end so everyone in the class can hear the flow of information.

▲ **Student Reproducibles**

Different Types of Paragraphs: Provide each student with a copy of this Different Types of Paragraphs reproducible for them to keep in their notebook. Review the four types of paragraphs included on the graphic organizer: expository, descriptive, persuasive, and narrative. Remind them that all paragraphs are alike in that they are a group of sentences about one main idea.

What Am I?: Have students use the Different Types of Paragraphs reproducible to determine each paragraph type presented on this page. Encourage them to point out specific features from each paragraph that support their conclusions.

Order! Order!: You may want to have small groups of students work together to complete the reproducible. Encourage them to jot ideas on separate sheets of paper as they read the sentences. Remind students to look for a beginning sentence that presents a main idea and an ending sentence that reinforces the idea. Another key point for students is to link sentences that are related. Some students may find it helpful to cut apart the sentences and physically rearrange them. Finally, to sharpen students' response to the flow of the paragraph, explain how helpful it can be to read aloud combinations of sentences. Ask volunteers to choose two or three related sentences to read aloud.

▲ Writing Practice

Gather a variety of high-interest short articles from magazines and newspapers. Duplicate the articles and cut apart the paragraphs. Store two articles in one envelope. Then challenge pairs of students to put the articles back together, paragraph by paragraph. They can glue the articles onto separate sheets of paper. To extend the practice, have partners rewrite the articles without indenting the paragraphs. Let pairs exchange articles and rewrite them with paragraph breaks. Discuss students' responses to reading the unindented paragraphs.

Name _____   Date _____

Different Types of Paragraphs

This graphic organizer describes the four different types of paragraphs.

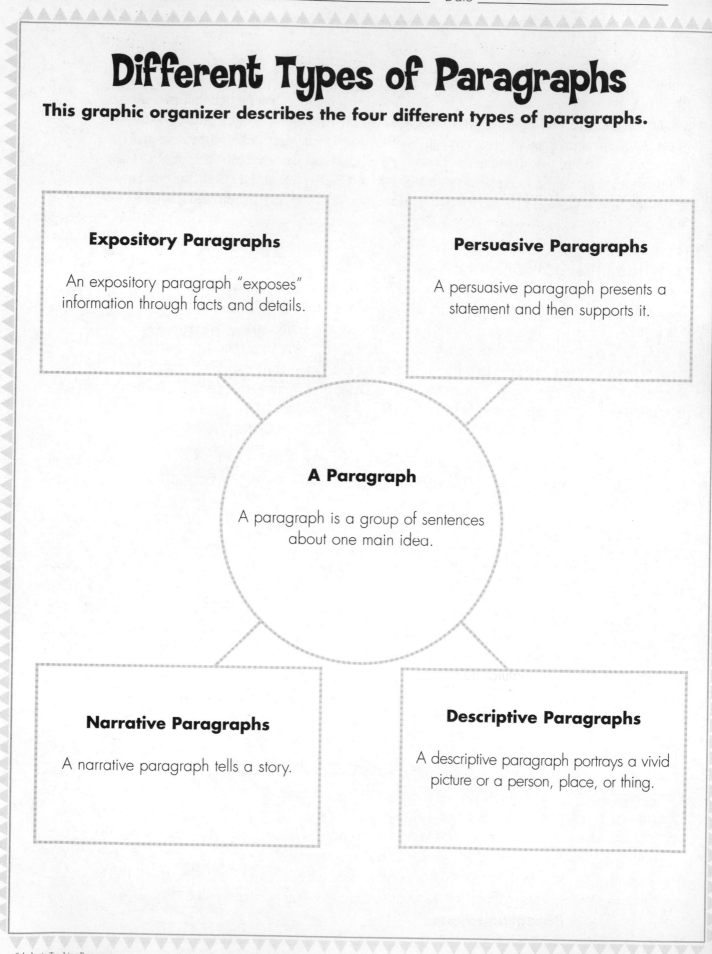

Expository Paragraphs

An expository paragraph "exposes" information through facts and details.

Persuasive Paragraphs

A persuasive paragraph presents a statement and then supports it.

A Paragraph

A paragraph is a group of sentences about one main idea.

Narrative Paragraphs

A narrative paragraph tells a story.

Descriptive Paragraphs

A descriptive paragraph portrays a vivid picture or a person, place, or thing.

What Am I?

Read each paragraph below. Decide if it is a narrative, expository, persuasive, or descriptive paragraph.

1.   Even though the tugboat is a small boat, it has big jobs to perform. For example, the tugboat helps to push and pull huge freighters and ocean liners in and out of city harbors. It helps maneuver large ships into their docks. Also, it pulls barges in and out of the harbor and along the coast. The tugboat, though small, is very powerful.
        Paragraph type: _____

2.   The Arctic polar bear is a large and formidable hunter. This enormous animal has huge hairy paws, long sharp claws, and powerful canine teeth. Its huge seven-foot body is covered with thick white hair. When the Arctic polar bear hunts a seal, first it silently pads up to the seal hole in the ice, waiting patiently for the seal to stick its head out of the water. Then, with a powerful blow of its huge paw, the bear kills its prey, drags it out of the hole, and tears its flesh with its powerful teeth. The polar bear is the largest of all bears.
        Paragraph type: _____

3.   Luke thought he'd be a natural when it came to snowboarding. After all, he'd been skateboarding and skiing for years. How different could it be? All it took was one trip, one very bumpy trip, down the slope to see that it was different. He had been excited as he rode up the chairlift to the top of the Double-Cross ski trail. Conditions were perfect: it was bright and sunny, and a fresh layer of snow covered everything. Luke was ready. Feeling exhilarated, he pushed off, headed down the slope, and fell immediately. None of his skiing or skateboarding experience had prepared him for this! He just couldn't maintain his balance. It was a long trip down to the bottom. Wet and frustrated, he was ready to give up. Just then, his friend Melinda snowboarded to his side. "I saw you coming down the slope," she said. "Want some pointers?" Melinda showed him how to maintain his balance and maneuver down the slope. After his fifth time down, Luke felt ecstatic. He wasn't the natural he'd hoped to be, but Melinda had put him on the road—or slope—to snowboard success.
        Paragraph type: _____

4.   To what extent should drivers of all-terrain vehicles determine how our woodlands are used? This is a question that concerns all of us who like to explore the Catskill Mountains. Here at the Mountain Post, we believe that our forests and hills attract residents and tourists who like hiking through the wild, untouched beauty and silence of the woods and hills. We feel that all-terrain vehicles destroy these attractions. The vehicles are noisy. Drivers cut muddy paths through forests, destroying plants and frightening animals away. The question of access to our woodlands is currently before our state legislators. We urge all of you who love the wildness of our mountains to write to our state representatives. Urge them to conserve our hills by prohibiting vehicles.
        Paragraph type: _____

Name _____   Date _____

Order! Order!

Place the sentences in order to create a paragraph. Write the number 1 beside the first sentence, and so on. Then rewrite the paragraph on another sheet of paper.

Living in the Desert

- These muscles enable the animal to carry heavy loads for long distances. _____

- At a gallop, racing camels can do 12 miles per hour. _____

- The hump is a mound of fatty tissue that can shrink. _____

- A camel's legs are long and thin, but they are very muscular. _____

- For instance, a camel can carry almost 1,000 pounds, but a load of about 400 pounds is the best weight. _____

- If no food is available, a camel gets energy from this fatty tissue. _____

- The typical distance a camel can walk each day is 25 miles. _____

- When a camel walks, the pads of its feet spread. _____

- With its hump and long legs, the camel may look funny, but it's uniquely suited to living in the desert. _____

- A walking camel travels about 3 miles per hour. _____

- Many people think that a camel's hump is filled with water, but this isn't true. _____

- This keeps the camel's feet from sinking into the sand. _____

- The lack of food in a desert and its soft, sandy surface are no problems for a camel! _____

The Structure of a Paragraph

◆ Purpose ◆

To introduce the parts of a paragraph

Before students can write a coherent and engaging paragraph, they must have an understanding of its structure. It's very easy for beginning writers—and even those who are experienced—to wander off the topic. Understanding the role of the topic sentence and the concluding sentence will help students focus on their subject. Recognizing that the body of a paragraph contains detail sentences that support the topic sentence will enable students to weed out unnecessary information that may creep into their work. And finally, using transition words and phrases will make their writing smoother and more logical.

▲ Launching Activity:
The Structure of a Paragraph (Overhead 2)

Now that students know what a paragraph is, they can move on to explore its structure.

Begin by reading aloud the paragraph or asking a volunteer to do so. Then use the questions at the bottom of the overhead to discuss the paragraph. You'll be able to mine your students' answers as you introduce structure later.

Then remind students that "The Midnight Ride of Sybil Luddington" is an expository paragraph, but that all types of paragraphs share the same structure. Label and identify each part of the paragraph on the overhead as they appear on the reproducible on page 13, A Paragraph up Close and Personal: title, topic sentence, transition words and phrases, detail sentences, body, and concluding sentence. Then explain each part. Be sure to refer to the comments your students made in your earlier discussion of the paragraph. For instance, you might say something like the following about the title: *The title of a paragraph is important because it gives a clue as to what the paragraph will be about. It should also draw in the reader so he or she will want to know more. Remember when Max said the title made him think of Paul Revere and his midnight ride? He was curious if the paragraph was about another event that happened during the American Revolution. Since Max is really interested in that topic, he was eager to read the paragraph.*

National Language Arts Standards:

▲ Recognizes a paragraph as a group of sentences about one main idea

▲ Uses prewriting strategies to plan written work

Overhead Transparency

◆ The Structure of a Paragraph

Reproducibles

◆ A Paragraph up Close and Personal

◆ Outlining Your Paragraph

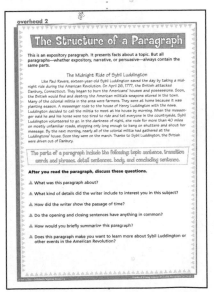

▲ Student Reproducibles

Make extra copies of both reproducibles for students to keep in their notebooks.

A Paragraph up Close and Personal: This reproducible labels the parts of the paragraph shown on The Structure of a Paragraph overhead. Remind students to refer to it as they write their own paragraphs.

Outlining Your Paragraph: To check students' comprehension of the parts of a paragraph, have them work backward. Display The Structure of a Paragraph overhead, without the parts labeled. Then ask students to identify the essential parts of the paragraph and write them on the reproducible. You can extend the use of this reproducible by having students identify the parts of other complete paragraphs from magazines or encyclopedia entries. Since there aren't enough lines on the reproducible to include all the details in the body, have students include the ones they feel are the most important

▲ Writing Practice

Brainstorm a list of potential expository paragraph topics with students. Although you may have to kick-start the discussion, encourage students to contribute topics that really interest them. At this point, the topics may be broad, such as Birds or Peregrine Falcons. The next lesson, Topic Sentences and Detail Sentences, will give you ideas on how to help students narrow their focus to create strong topic sentences.

A Paragraph up Close and Personal

Although paragraphs may have different subjects, they all share the same structure.

Title: tells about the subject of the para-graph and interests the reader

The Midnight Ride of Sybil Luddington

Transition word: helps connect the sentences in the paragraph

Topic sentence: tells what the paragraph will be about (usually the first sentence or a sentence near the beginning of the para-graph)

Like Paul Revere, sixteen-year-old Sybil Luddington saved the day by taking a midnight ride during the American Revolution. On April 26, 1777, the British attacked Danbury, Connecticut. They began to burn the Americans' houses and possessions. **Soon**, the British would find and destroy the American militia's weapons stored in the town. Many of the colonial militia in the area were farmers. They were at home because it was planting season. A messenger rode to the house of Henry Luddington with the news. Luddington decided to call the militia to meet at his house by morning. When the messenger said he and his horse were too tired to ride and tell everyone in the countryside, Sybil Luddington volunteered to go. In the darkness of night, she rode for more than forty miles on mostly unfamiliar roads, stopping only long enough to bang on shutters and shout her message. **By the next morning,** nearly all of the colonial militia had gathered at the Luddingtons' house. Soon they were on the march. **Thanks to Sybil Luddington, the British were driven out of Danbury.**

Body (sentences 2–11): contains the detail sentences

Transition phrase: gives a sense of time and order of events

Concluding sentence: wraps up the topic sentence (usually the last sentence in the paragraph)

Name _____   Date _____

Outlining Your Paragraph

The Topic Is: _____

Title: _____

Topic Sentence: _____

_____

Body

Detail: _____

_____

Detail: _____

_____

Detail: _____

_____

Detail: _____

_____

Detail: _____

_____

Detail: _____

_____

Concluding Sentence: _____

_____

Transition Words and Phrases I Can Use: _____

_____

Topic Sentences and Detail Sentences

◆ Purpose ◆

To explore the role of a topic sentence in a paragraph and to show how the other sentences support it

Now that you've taught the structure of a paragraph to your students, you can focus more attention on each of its parts, beginning with the topic sentence. A good topic sentence gives a writer ideas to explore and develop. Students who are working with a poorly defined topic sentence will find it difficult to write a well-developed paragraph. For example, if a paragraph begins with an overly general topic sentence, each detail may support the topic sentence without relating to one another at all.

Also, we as teachers must be aware of how we present topics to our students. Throwing out a direction such as "Write about George Washington" can be overwhelming because many students have difficulty settling on a logical starting point.

▲ Launching Activity:
Topic Sentences and Detail Sentences (Overhead 3)

Before displaying the overhead, write the topic, hamburger, on the board. Then show students how to develop a question to create a topic sentence. Present a scenario like the following to your class: *If someone said to me, "Write a paragraph about the hamburger," I think I'd have a hard time deciding exactly what to write about. To help me make up my mind, I'd begin to think about what kinds of questions I have about hamburgers. For instance, I wonder how the hamburger got its name."* Then write the question *How did the hamburger get its name?* on the board. Elicit questions about the hamburger from students and write them on the board.

Then show the overhead to students. Point out the similarity between the question you wrote on the board and the title of the paragraph, and how the topic sentence indicates that the paragraph will answer your question. Allow time for students to rephrase one of the questions on the board to create a title and possible topic sentence, and discuss their work.

National Language Arts Standards:

▲ Recognizes a paragraph as a group of sentences about one main idea

▲ Uses paragraph form in writing

Overhead Transparency

◆ Topic Sentences and Detail Sentences

Reproducible

◆ Getting Off to a Good Start

---

overhead 3

Topic Sentences and Detail Sentences

A strong topic sentence gets your paragraph off to a great start, but sometimes you have to narrow down the topic.

Topic: The Hamburger
↓
A Question I Have About the Hamburger:
How did the hamburger get its name?
↓
Paragraph

How the Hamburger Got Its Name

It's unclear who actually cooked the first hamburger, but the origins of the sandwich's name can be traced. Mongolian tribes led by Genghis Khan shredded and ate beef from poor-quality cows because it was easier to digest. After being invaded by the Mongolians, Russians began eating ground meat, too. Then German ships visiting Russian ports discovered the delicacy. Soon, cooked ground meat became known as "Hamburg steak" after the German city of Hamburg. German immigrants introduced the Hamburg steak to America. Someone—it may have been Charlie Nagreen of Seymour, Wisconsin; Fletcher Davis of Athens, Texas; Charles and Franck Menches of Hamburg, New York; or Louis Lassen of New Haven, Connecticut—turned the Hamburg steak into a sandwich by placing it between two slices of bread. The hamburger was born.

A **topic sentence** tells what the paragraph will be about.

▲ The topic sentence appears at or near the beginning of the paragraph.
▲ A good topic sentence—and title—spark a reader's interest.
▲ Detail sentences support the topic sentence.

What kinds of questions do you have about the hamburger? How can you turn your question into a title and a topic sentence?

Question: _____

Title: _____

Possible Topic Sentence: _____

▲ Student Reproducible

Getting Off to a Good Start: The two paragraphs on this reproducible will help students see how a vague topic sentence can make a writer wander all around a subject without giving the reader any substantive information. As students work, walk around the room to monitor their progress. Some pupils may find it difficult at first to articulate the reasons for choosing one paragraph over the other. To challenge students, ask them to provide exciting new titles for the paragraphs.

▲ Writing Practice

Find a few paragraphs that have compelling topic sentences. Write one paragraph on the board each day, but omit the topic sentence. After students read the paragraph, challenge them to supply the missing topic sentence. Ask volunteers to write their topic sentences on the board, and have them explain how they developed the sentences. Assist them in refining their sentences as necessary. You also may want to supply your own somewhat general topic sentence and ask students to guide you in making it stronger. Then compare the original topic sentences to the ones you and your class created, and discuss the differences.

Getting Off to a Good Start

Which paragraph is more powerful? Read both of them and decide.
Explain your choice.

Making Stickers Is Easy

It's easy to make your own stickers. You can use pictures from magazines or draw your own pictures to turn into stickers. You can make a mixture out of boiling water and gelatin and brush it on the back of the picture. Be careful! Make sure you have an adult with you! Or you can mix white glue and vinegar and use that as glue. You can also use fabric paint to draw a design on a mirror or a jar lid and let it dry. As you can see, there are many, many ways to make stickers yourself.

Quick, Easy, and Cheap Stickers

You can make your own stickers at home or school by following these instructions. Begin by cutting out pictures from magazines to turn into stickers or drawing and cutting out your own pictures. Next, mix together two parts of white glue with one part of white vinegar, and add a few drops of peppermint extract. Then brush the mixture on the back of your stickers. After they dry, lick the glue side (tastes like peppermint) and press on the stickers. In no time at all—and for very little money—you can make dozens of cool and unique stickers.

Title of the more powerful paragraph: _____

I think it is more powerful because: _____

_____

_____

_____

_____

Developing a Paragraph

National Language Arts Standards:

▲ Recognizes a paragraph as a group of sentences about one main idea

▲ Establishes coherence within paragraphs

Overhead Transparency

◆ Developing a Paragraph

Reproducibles

◆ Building a Paragraph

◆ How Is a Paragraph Like a Hamburger?

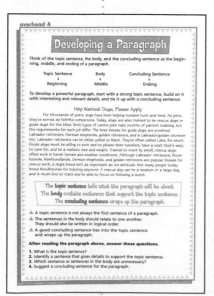

◆ Purpose ◆

To establish how to develop a cohesive paragraph

Once students understand how to create a good topic sentence, you can show them how to develop a paragraph that flows and is cohesive. The secret to a well-developed paragraph is organization. As the previous lesson pointed out, a weak topic sentence encourages a writer to meander. Consequently, the body of the paragraph may not flow because the details aren't linked.

When students write paragraphs, encourage them to refer to the following reproducibles: A Paragraph up Close and Personal (page 13), Outlining Your Paragraph (page 14), and How Is a Paragraph Like a Hamburger? (page 21) to organize their material.

▲ Launching Activity: Developing a Paragraph (Overhead 4)

After sharing the information about developing a paragraph on the overhead, allow time for students to read "Help Wanted: Dogs, Please Apply" independently. Then go over the questions at the bottom of the overhead. You may want to start by modeling a partial response to the first question: *After reading the paragraph, I realized that the first sentence isn't the topic sentence. It's too general and doesn't tell what the paragraph is really about. And the rest of the sentences don't support it. However, this first sentence does lead to or build up to the topic sentence.*

Then elicit students' reactions to the second sentence. Call on other students to read sentences that support the topic sentence. Then, as the class responds to the third question, cross out the irrelevant sentences in the paragraph. Challenge students to explain why these sentences are unnecessary. Finally, collaborate with students to compose a satisfying concluding sentence.

Answers: 1. Third sentence: Today, dogs are also trained to be rescue dogs or guide dogs for the blind. 2. Accept any sentence except for those shown in the answer for question 3. 3. Sixth sentence: Labrador retrievers can be either yellow or black. Seventh sentence: They're often called Labs for short. Eleventh sentence: Not many people today breed bloodhounds for tracking anymore. 4. Sample answer: Whether a person wants a companion, is looking for a rescue dog, or has special needs, there is most likely a dog that can be trained to do the job.

▲ Student Reproducibles

Building a Paragraph: In this reproducible, students create their own paragraphs by selecting a topic, details for the body, and a concluding sentence. Encourage students to rephrase and move the sentences as necessary to create a cohesive paragraph.

How Is a Paragraph Like a Hamburger?: Since many students are visual learners, this model may enable them to better visualize the parts of a paragraph. You may want to use this reproducible in conjunction with the overhead. This will give students an opportunity to familiarize themselves with it. Then distribute additional copies so students can keep them in their notebooks.

▲ Writing Practice

In the previous lesson, students brainstormed topics about the hamburger. Now ask them to research the topic and write a paragraph about it. Remind them to outline the paragraph. After completing their work, students can use the hamburger graphic organizer (page 21) to assess the development of the paragraph.

▲ Enriching the Lesson

"Help Wanted: Dogs, Please Apply" is an example of an expository paragraph that compares and contrasts information. To extend the lesson, draw a Venn diagram on the board. Have students supply a title for each circle and then help you fill in the diagram. For additional writing practice, ask students to write a paragraph comparing and contrasting summer and winter or spring and fall.

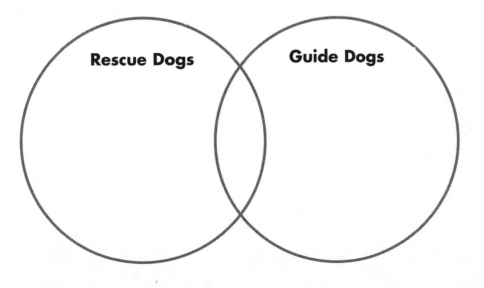

Building a Paragraph

Build a paragraph by choosing a topic sentence, at least three detail sentences for the body, and a concluding sentence. Circle your choices. Then write your paragraph on another sheet of paper. To make your paragraph flow, you may rewrite or reorder some of the sentences.

Possible Topic Sentence: (Choose one.)

- Americans seem to love watermelon.
- Some American towns are crazy about watermelon.
- What do Green River, Utah; Dilley, Texas; Luling, Texas; and Hope, Arkansas, have in comon?
- Several American cities bill themselves as the "Watermelon Capital"—and they have the watermelons to prove it.

Possible Detail Sentences: (Choose at least three.)

- Hope, Arkansas, has produced watermelons that weigh more than 100 pounds.
- The water tower in Hope is in the shape of a watermelon.
- President Bill Clinton was born in Hope, Arkansas.
- Green River, Utah, sports a giant watermelon statue that is 25 feet long.
- The Utah watermelon statue even has a motor, but it's broken, so the statue doesn't move anymore.
- In Green River, the watermelon statue is hollow.
- Another town with a watermelon-shaped water tower is Luling, Texas.
- Every summer, Luling hosts the Watermelon Thump.
- Luling paints its oil pumps.
- The Watermelon Thump features a car rally and a watermelon-seed-spitting contest.
- Although about 15 million watermelons are harvested in Dilley, Texas, each year, its watermelon statue is only 5 feet long.
- Dilley's watermelon statue is in the city park.
- The watermelon harvest in Dilley begins in June.
- The slogan of Dilley is "Self-Proclaimed Watermelon Capital of Texas."

Possible Concluding Sentence: (Choose one.)

- Lincoln, Illinois, named after Abraham Lincoln, also has a watermelon monument.
- Visitors to Bald Knob, Arkansas, may see a giant watermelon statue on the back of a roadside truck.
- There may not be one "Watermelon Capital," but many towns enjoy celebrating this sweet and juicy fruit.
- To truly represent itself as the "Watermelon Capital," a town has to build a watermelon statue or monument.

How Is a Paragraph Like a Hamburger?

Think of the top bun as the topic sentence, the meat and vegetables as the details that form the body, and the bottom bun as the concluding sentence. Use this graphic organizer to help you develop a powerful paragraph.

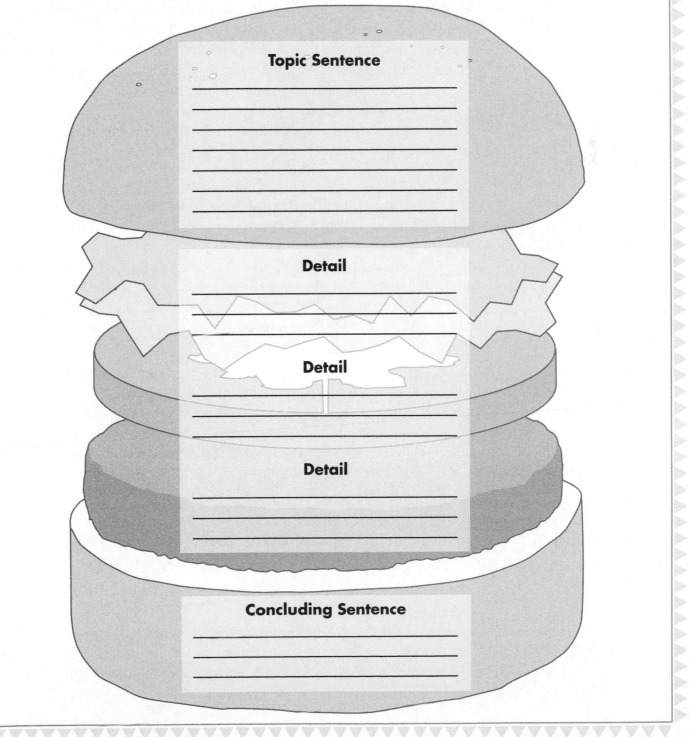

Topic Sentence

Detail

Detail

Detail

Concluding Sentence

Transitions

National Language Arts Standards:

▲ Recognizes a paragraph as a group of sentences about one main idea

▲ Establishes coherence within paragraphs

Overhead Transparency

◆ Transitions

Reproducibles

◆ A Handy List of Transition Words and Phrases

◆ Lost in Transition

◆ Purpose ◆

To demonstrate how transitional words and phrases link the sentences in a paragraph

Although students may understand how to develop a paragraph, their paragraphs may read and sound more like a list of sentences rather than a cohesive group of sentences. Their paragraphs often are missing transitional words and phrases that help the sentences flow more naturally from one idea to another. Many students often confuse transitions; for instance, they might use a transition word to emphasize an idea when they mean to conclude or summarize. And in their enthusiasm, it can be common for students to overuse transitional words. With some gentle encouragement and guidance on your part, young writers can recognize how to use transitions more economically and effectively.

▲ Launching Activity: Transitions (Overhead 5)

After sharing the information about transitions on the overhead, ask students if they can identify transition words and phrases in "Marbles on the Move." Record the transition words on the board, and then see if students can identify the type of each transition. Distribute the reproducible A Handy List of Transition Words and Phrases so students can check their answers. Allow time for them to point out any transitions they might have missed.

Then work with students to create a coherent and logical paragraph from the sentences at the bottom of the overhead. To get them started, read aloud the sentences, and ask students what the paragraph would be about. You may want to model your own response: *I think we could transform these sentences into a strong paragraph about how to make lemonade. The sentences seem to be arranged in a logical order, so all we need to do is add transitions to make them flow together.*

Allow time for students to look over the completed paragraph. Also read aloud the paragraph so they can hear how it sounds. This will give students the opportunity to evaluate their work and make any changes.

▲ Student Reproducibles

A Handy List of Transition Words and Phrases: Distribute a copy to each student to store in his or her notebook as an easy reference. You may want to select a few brief paragraphs that include transitional words for the class to study and keep as samples. Also, urge students to look out for transitional words when they read and to add them to the list.

Lost in Transition: Make sure students have their list of transition words and phrases handy. Before they begin to write the paragraph, encourage them to think about its purpose. Will it explain how to do something? Will it be comparing or contrasting information? Will it be presenting a sequence of events?

▲ Writing Practice

Create a series of how-to topics for simple, everyday tasks, such as tying a shoe, brushing one's teeth, setting a table, directions to the classroom from the school's front entrance, and so on. Let each student choose a topic, or make up an appropriate topic, and then write a short, expository paragraph describing the steps in the process. Emphasize the importance of transitional words, and point out that a paragraph may contain more than one type of transitional word. Ask pairs of students to exchange paragraphs and critique their effectiveness. Did each writer make good use of transitions?

A Handy List of
Transition Words and Phrases
This chart shows some of the variety of transition words and phrases.

To Show Time

about	during	meanwhile	third	until
after	first	next week	till	yesterday
as soon as	immediately	second	today	
at	in the meantime	soon	tomorrow	
before	later	then		

To Show Location

above	around	beside	in front of	on top of
across	away	between	inside	onto
against	back	beyond	into	outside
along	behind	by	near	over
amid	below	down	of	throughout
among	beneath	from	off	under

To Compare

also	at	in the same way	like	similarly

To Contrast

although	conversely	however	on the contrary	otherwise
but	counter to	nevertheless	on the other hand	yet

To Add Information

additionally	and	finally	in addition	next
again	another	for example	likewise	together with
along with	as well	for instance	moreover	
also	besides	furthermore		

To Emphasize an Idea

again	in fact	to emphasize	truly	with this in mind
for this reason	indeed	to repeat		

To Conclude or Summarize

accordingly	consequently	in conclusion	therefore	to sum up
all in all	due to	in summary	thus	
as a result	finally			

Lost in Transition

Turn the information below into a paragraph. Think about how to use transition words to link the ideas. Write your paragraph on the lines below and feel free to rewrite the tips.

Lost in the Wild

Have you ever thought about what might happen if you got lost in the desert, mountains, or forest? Here are some tips.

- Tell someone where you are going.
- Carry a map and a compass. Know how to use them.
- Carry a backpack with a first-aid kit, extra food and clothing, sunglasses, and a flashlight.
- Wear a whistle around your neck. Blow it three times if you get lost.
- You may have to start a fire. You'll need matches (waterproof) or a lighter.
- Think you're lost? Don't keep walking. This might make it more difficult for rescuers to find you.
- Stay calm. Don't panic. It could cause you to become confused.
- Wait for help. Eat a meal. Set up your tent.
- Remember that people will be looking for you.

_____

_____

_____

_____

_____

_____

_____

_____

_____

_____

Expository Paragraphs

National Language Arts Standards:

▲ Recognizes a paragraph as a group of sentences about one main idea

▲ Uses strategies to write for different audiences and to write for a variety of purposes

▲ Writes expository compositions

Overhead Transparency

◆ Expository Paragraphs

Reproducibles

◆ Sequence

◆ Cause and Effect

◆ Compare and Contrast

◆ Problem and Solution

◆ **Purpose** ◆ To introduce the different types of expository paragraphs and their purposes

During their school years, students are exposed to expository paragraphs more than any other type of paragraph. Their textbooks are filled with expository paragraphs that present information in a factual manner. As students encounter more varieties of printed material, they'll need to have the skills to recognize how that material is being presented. For instance, is the author setting forth facts or opinions? To become effective writers, students must be able understand their goals in writing and to identify their audience.

▲ **Launching Activity: Expository Paragraphs (Overhead 6)**

After reading aloud "Is There Enough Pizza for Leftovers?" to students, have them point out the facts in the paragraph. Then ask if they spot any opinions or personal information that the author may have included. Explain that the paragraph is an example of an expository paragraph because it "exposes" information about the topic of record-breaking pizzas in the United States. (Note that the paragraph is not strictly compare-contrast or problem-solution but a combination.)

Then share the information about expository paragraphs on the overhead. To illustrate examples of the different types of expository paragraphs, you can refer to the following pages: sequence—"Quick, Easy, and Cheap Stickers," page 17; cause and effect—"How the Hamburger Got Its Name," overhead 3; compare and contrast—"Help Wanted: Dogs, Please Apply," overhead 4; and problem and solution—"The Midnight Ride of Sybil Luddington," page 13.

Work through the exercises at the bottom of the overhead with students. Make sure they understand that exercise 2 is not part of an expository paragraph; neither the title nor the first sentence contain any facts. On the other hand, 1 and 3 are clearly factual. At this point, you may want to share and discuss the information in Enriching the Lesson with students.

▲ **Student Reproducibles**

Keep a store of these reproducibles in a writing center so students can have easy access to the graphic organizers.

---

overhead 6

Expository Paragraphs

Your teacher says, "Write a paragraph about one of these topics: how to make a pizza, the history of pizza in the United States, Italian pizza versus American pizza, or the largest pizza ever made. And stick to the facts, please." No matter which topic you choose, you'll be writing an expository paragraph.

Is There Enough Pizza for Leftovers?

The United States has had its share of huge pizzas. The largest pizza in the United States was created in Havana, Florida. It weighed 44,457 pounds—including 18,174 pounds of flour; 1,103 pounds of water; 6,446 pounds of sauce; 9,375 pounds of cheese; and 2,387 pounds of pepperoni. After being cut into 94,248 slices, the pizza was served to more than 30,000 people in Mt. Pleasant, Iowa, people can buy their own record-breaking pizza. This pizza measures 4 feet in diameter, which translates into 1,814 square inches of pie. It took several tries for the owners of the pizzeria to get the pie right. The first pizza stuck to the bottom of the pan, so they added cornmeal to the crust and changed the oven temperatures. After about 20 minutes, a pizza with eight pounds of cheese, 64 ounces of sauce, and 170 ounces of dough comes out of the oven. (It has to be taken out of the oven by two people.) No matter how—or where—you slice it, that's a lot of pizza!

An **expository paragraph** presents facts about a topic. There are different types of expository paragraphs.

▲ An expository paragraph can present information in sequence.
▲ An expository paragraph can show cause and effect.
▲ An expository paragraph can compare and contrast information.
▲ An expository paragraph can explain a problem and how it was solved.

Read the titles and first sentences of each paragraph below. Which paragraphs will be expository? How can you tell?

1. Title: "The Connection Between World War II and American Pizza"
First sentence: During World War II in Italy, Italian soldiers ate their first pizza.

2. Title: "Why I Don't Like Mushrooms on My Pizza"
First sentence: I never order mushrooms on my pizza because they make the crust soggy.

3. Title: "Tomatoes Make the Pizza"
First sentence: The first tomatoes were brought to Europe from Peru and Ecuador in the 1500s, but Europeans believed they were poisonous.

Sequence: Remind students that sequencing can involve the timing of events or following steps.

Cause and Effect: To help differentiate between cause and effect, students can use the following questions: What happened? (effect) and Why did it happen? (cause)

Compare and Contrast: Emphasize that similarities are written in the overlapping sections of the two circles.

Problem and Solution: Make sure students understand that a problem may have more than one solution, or that it may take several attempts to reach a solution. The result is what occurs when the problem is finally resolved.

▲ Writing Practice

Assign one of the topics at the top of the Expository Paragraphs overhead: how to make a pizza, the history of pizza in the United States, Italian pizza versus American pizza, or the largest pizza ever made. Encourage students to use the graphic organizers on pages 28–31 to help them organize information. After students are satisfied with their work, share the paragraphs during a pizza party. They'll have a new appreciation for pizza— and for expository paragraphs.

▲ Enriching the Lesson

Have your students noticed that the expository paragraphs in this book are written in the third person? Because expository paragraphs are factual, the third-person voice lends more objectivity to the writing. Using the first-person voice in an expository paragraph may focus unwarranted attention on the writer, distract the reader from the topic, and lead to wordiness. Explain to students that the point of view of the author is implied by the topic and facts of an expository paragraph. Tell students that they'll be studying other types of paragraphs—narrative, descriptive, and persuasive—where the first-person point of view may be essential to the understanding of the writing.

Sequence

Expository paragraphs sometimes explain a sequence of events, for example, the biography of Geronimo. In expository paragraphs that tell how to do something, the sequence of steps is important. You can use this chart to help you organize the sequence of events or steps to include in an expository paragraph.

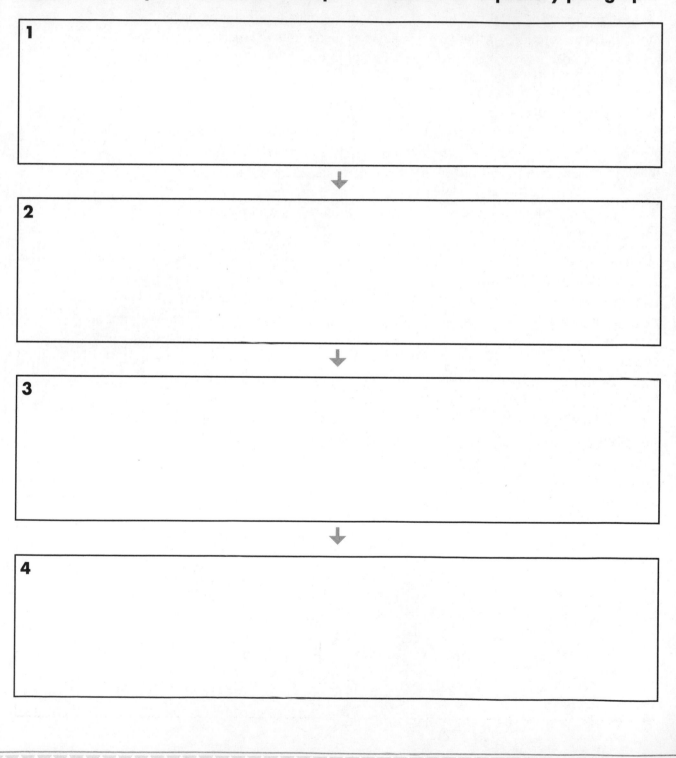

Name _____ Date _____

Cause and Effect

An expository paragraph can explain what happened (effect) and why it happened (cause). You can use this chart to help you organize the causes and effects to include in an expository paragraph.

Cause   **Effect**

Compare and Contrast

An expository paragraph can show how people, places, or things are similar and different. You can use a Venn diagram to organize the similarities and differences to include in an expository paragraph.

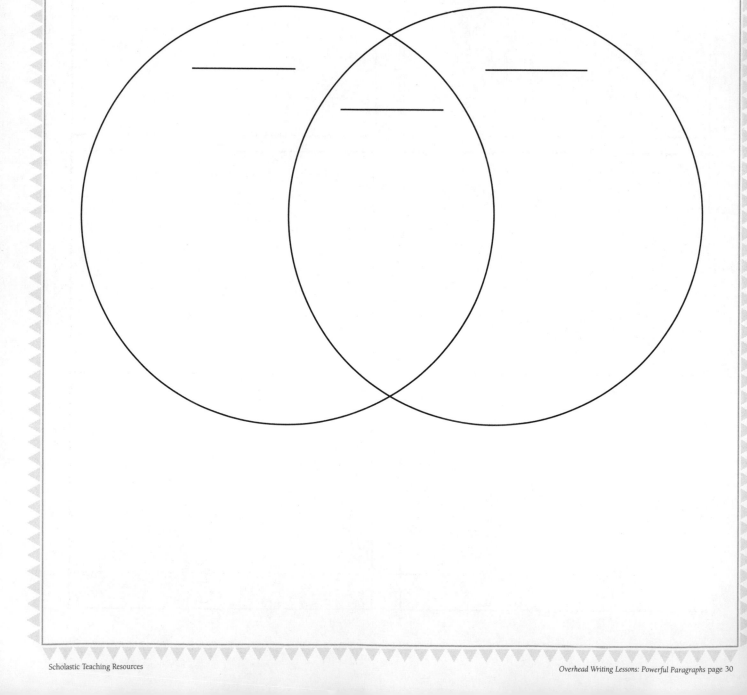

Problem and Solution

An expository paragraph can focus on a problem and how it was solved. You can use this chart to help you organize problems and solutions to include in an expository paragraph.

Problem(s)

Solution(s)

Result(s)

Narrative Paragraphs

National Language Arts Standards:

▲ Recognizes a paragraph as a group of sentences about one main idea

▲ Uses strategies to write for different audiences and to write for a variety of purposes

▲ Writes narrative accounts

Overhead Transparency

◆ Narrative Paragraphs

Reproducible

◆ Getting Ready to Write a Narrative Paragraph

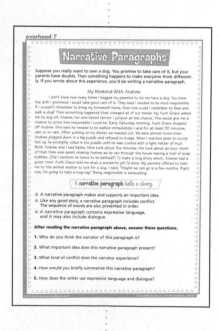

◆ Purpose ◆

To introduce the narrative paragraph and distinguish it from the expository paragraph

So far in the book, students have been exposed to examples of expository paragraphs. Now it's time to turn their attention to other types of paragraphs, beginning with the narrative paragraph. When students narrate personal experiences, they often slip into a stream-of-consciousness mode. Instead of producing a well-structured narrative, their writing meanders. By introducing the distinct elements of narrative paragraphs and also re-emphasizing that all paragraphs have the same structure, you'll give your students a solid framework expressing themselves.

▲ Launching Activity: Narrative Paragraphs (Overhead 7)

Before beginning this activity, look for examples of narrative paragraphs told from the third-person point of view. For instance, many textbooks have sections that rely on narrative paragraphs rather than expository paragraphs to engage students' interest. It's important to stress to students that narrative paragraphs are more than first-person accounts.

Share the elements of the narrative paragraph given on the overhead. Then ask a volunteer to read aloud "My Weekend With Andrew." After a brief, general discussion about the paragraph, ask students to read the paragraph independently and then answer the questions at the bottom of the overhead with them. Here is an example of how you might guide responses to the first question: *Who do you think is telling this story? Do any clues indicate how old this person might be? Do you know whether a male or a female is telling the story?* Students should realize that the narrator could be about their age because he or she can't get a pet without parental permission.

Sample responses: 2. Idea: The narrator realizes that the reality of taking care of a dog is a bigger job than he or she thought it would be. 3. Conflict: The narrator has to prove that he or she is responsible enough to take care of a pet. 4. Summary: The narrator wants to own a pet, but his or her parents say no. After proving that he or she is responsible by successfully dog sitting, the parents say the narrator can have a dog. Now that the narrator knows what a big job owning a dog can be, he or she decides to wait a while. 5. Language: "plopped in a big puddle," "coated with a light batter of mud"; dialogue: The author quotes her- or himself at the end of the paragraph.

▲ Student Reproducible

Getting Ready to Write a Narrative Paragraph: Go over each element in the graphic organizer. Explain to students that they may not need to have dialogue for each event. To familiarize students with the reproducible, have them use it to break down the paragraph "My Weekend With Andrew" from the overhead. Distribute several copies of the reproducible for them to keep in their notebooks, and place extra copies in the writing center. Students also will use the reproducible to help them complete the Writing Practice activity.

▲ Writing Practice

Challenge students to think of a personal experience they could translate into a narrative paragraph. Remind them that the experience must make a point instead of merely relating a sequence of events. Have students begin by filling out the Getting Ready to Write a Narrative Paragraph reproducible on page 34. Stress that they may have to discard several experiences before they settle on one that effectively conveys an idea, and tell them they shouldn't get discouraged. Be on hand to consult with students and help them shape their narratives as needed.

Getting Ready
to Write a Narrative Paragraph

When you write a narrative paragraph, you're telling a story. You can use this chart to help you organize your thoughts before you write.

The Idea: _____

The Conflict: _____

Sequence of Events

1. _____

Details: _____

_____

Dialogue

2. _____

Details: _____

_____

Dialogue

3. _____

Details: _____

_____

Dialogue

4. _____

Details: _____

_____

Dialogue

Descriptive Paragraphs

◆ **Purpose** ◆

To introduce the descriptive paragraph and show how it appeals to the senses

Now that students have a good grasp of expository and narrative paragraphs, it's time to approach descriptive paragraphs. Students have learned that every paragraph has the same structure, and they're beginning to see how they can use the different types of paragraphs to reach different audiences. Learning to write good descriptive paragraphs will sharpen their senses and broaden their vocabulary.

▲ **Launching Activity: Descriptive Paragraphs (Overhead 8)**
Have students close their eyes and listen as you read aloud the descriptive paragraph by Stephen King on the overhead. Then ask them to tell you about what they experienced as you read. Did they picture the attic? Did they hear the "whoosh of the furnace" and the "patter of rats"? What kind of feeling did the paragraph give them? Then write the five senses on the board: Sight, Sound, Smell, Taste, and Touch. Discuss King's paragraph in terms of its sensory details; let students suggest details to list under the senses.

As you share the information about descriptive paragraphs on the overhead, give examples of types of descriptive paragraphs—memoirs or autobiographies such as King's, novels, and short stories. Like narrative writing, descriptive writing is often explained as "showing instead of telling." The reader is swept up in the events and details of the writing. The writer creates a mood, or feeling, through words.

Then turn to the exercise at the bottom of the page. You may want to record students' responses in a sensory list or a sensory word web (see page 37). Begin the exercise by contributing one or two details, such as the following for a slice of watermelon: *When I shut my eyes and think of a slice of watermelon, I immediately see its deep pink color and its black seeds. Then I think about how sweet and refreshing watermelon tastes on a hot summer day.*

As students volunteer more sensory details, add them to the list or word web. Work on the second topic as a class, too, but let students tackle the third topic by themselves. Point out that, for some topics, they might not be able to think of details for all five senses.

National Language Arts Standards:

▲ Recognizes a paragraph as a group of sentences about one main idea
▲ Uses sensory details

Overhead Transparency

◆ Descriptive Paragraphs

Reproducible

◆ Sensory Web

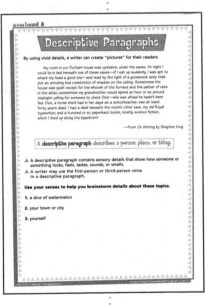

35

▲ Student Reproducible

Make extra copies of the Sensory Web reproducible for students to keep in their notebooks. Also store a few copies in your writing center.

To introduce the web, ask students to use it to describe the classroom. Divide the class into two groups. While one group is working on the reproducible, continue working with the other group. This will enable students to observe and experience the classroom in action so they can gather more sensory details.

▲ Writing Practice

Challenge students to write a descriptive paragraph about their classroom. Remind them to use their completed Sensory Web reproducible as a guide. They will still need to structure their paragraphs to include a title, a strong topic sentence, descriptive detail sentences, and a good concluding sentence. And in this case, their paragraphs should also convey a mood. Set aside time for students to share their writing. It will be enlightening for them—and you—to see the many diverse perspectives on the same room.

▲ Enriching the Lesson

Take the exploration of descriptive paragraphs a step further by making a comparative study of the opening paragraphs of two novels or stories. Do the paragraphs give readers a sense of the problems or conflicts the characters will face? What kind of mood do these first paragraphs evoke? This will get students thinking about how an opening paragraph relates to the work as a whole, and the similarities and differences between the works can lead to a discussion of style. Carol has used *Tuck Everlasting* by Natalie Babbitt and *Roll of Thunder, Hear My Cry* by Mildred Taylor with great success in her classroom. Each book begins on a hot day in the late summer, but the setting and the problems of the main characters are clearly different.

Sensory Web

A descriptive paragraph uses sensory details to paint a picture of a person, place, or thing. You can use a sensory word web to help you organize those details.

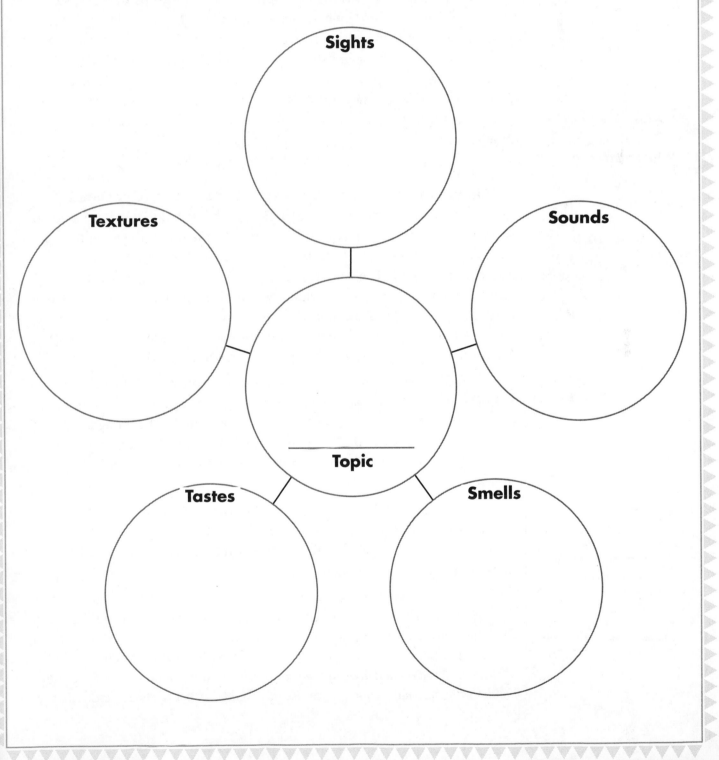

Persuasive Paragraphs

National Language Arts Standards:

▲ Recognizes a paragraph as a group of sentences about one main idea

▲ Writes persuasive composition subject

Overhead Transparency

◆ Persuasive Paragraphs

Reproducible

◆ Facts and More Facts

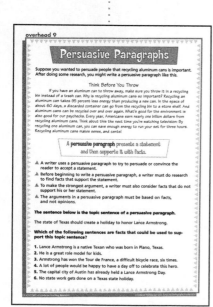

◆ **Purpose** ◆

To introduce the elements of a persuasive paragraph

After exploring how to incorporate their own responses and experiences through writing descriptive and narrative paragraphs, students now tackle persuasive paragraphs. They must learn to be rigorous in differentiating between facts and opinions. Like expository paragraphs, persuasive paragraphs involve researching facts. But in order to persuade readers to adopt a viewpoint, students have to go beyond the mere presentation of facts. They must also anticipate that some facts may not support their main statement and figure out how to address those arguments persuasively.

▲ **Launching Activity: Persuasive Paragraphs (Overhead 9)**

Quickly review the different types of paragraphs that students have studied so far: expository, descriptive, and narrative. Explain that they will now be learning about persuasive paragraphs, which, like expository paragraphs, are also research-based. The goal in writing a persuasive paragraph is to persuade someone to accept your views on a topic. Emphasize to students that they must rely on facts and not opinions to sway their readers. Have them define the difference between facts and opinions and give examples of each. Then share the information about persuasive paragraphs on the overhead.

Before reading aloud "Think Before You Throw," conduct a survey. Ask: *Do you think recycling aluminum cans is a good idea?* Then read and discuss the paragraph. Do students detect any opinions in the paragraph? What facts are presented? List these on the board. Did the writer do a persuasive job? Find out if the paragraph made any students change their minds about recycling.

Then answer the question at the bottom of the overhead. Students should recognize that sentences 1, 3, and 5 are facts that support the statement; that sentences 2 and 4 are opinions; and that sentence 6 is a fact that does not support the statement.

Students may struggle with the idea that a fact may not agree with their position. They may be tempted to discard it instead of using the fact as the basis for an argument. Model for students how you might counter sentence 6 in a persuasive paragraph: *The argument in sentence 6 is that state offices are closed on holidays and that no work gets done. I know that some state holidays are optional, so offices can decide whether or not to close. Cesar Chavez*

Day on March 31 is an optional holiday. I also know that some state offices are open and have a reduced staff on certain holidays, such as Lyndon Baines Johnson Day, celebrated on August 27. I would argue that Lance Armstrong Day could be an optional holiday or a reduced-staff holiday.

▲ Student Reproducible

Facts and More Facts: Distribute several copies of this reproducible for students to keep in their notebooks. Also place extra copies in the writing center. In order to familiarize students with the reproducible, ask them to write a brief persuasive paragraph supporting Lance Armstrong Day as a Texas holiday. Have them use the sentences at the bottom of the overhead, and encourage them to research more facts to include.

▲ Writing Practice

Extend the idea for the persuasive paragraph at the bottom of the overhead. Have students select a person to honor with a state or national holiday. This person may be famous or known only to the student. You may want to enlist the aid of the school or public librarian to help students undertake their research. Also make sure they're armed with the reproducible on page 40. After students complete their paragraphs, hold a conference with each one. Constructively point out any opinions that have crept into their work or any unnecessary or unsubstantiated facts. Then let students read one another's work and vote on the person they think is most deserving of a holiday.

Facts and More Facts

When you write a persuasive paragraph, rely on facts to convince your readers. Use this chart to help you organize your material.

My Statement: _____

_____

Facts That Support My Statement

Facts That Do Not Support My Statement

What Arguments Can I Make Against These Facts?

Editing and Proofreading Paragraphs

◆ Purpose ◆

To emphasize the importance of editing and proofreading one's own work

Students are often surprised to find that they haven't successfully translated the ideas in their heads onto the page. It often can be hard for them to see exactly what they've written. Going back to a piece of writing after several days helps sharpen their vision, as does allowing another student or the teacher to comment on their work. By understanding the different parts of a paragraph and how each is developed, students have built a strong foundation for their writing. But the final steps in any kind of writing are editing and proofreading.

▲ Launching Activity: Editing and Proofreading Paragraphs (Overhead 10)

Since you'll be working with students on editing and proofreading "A Very Bad Move" from Overhead 10, you may want to make a photocopy of the paragraph for each student to mark. Otherwise, you can make the changes directly on the overhead, or call up volunteers to do so.

After reading aloud "A Very Bad Move," go over the questions pages 47–48 at the bottom of the overhead with students. (Study the sample marked paragraph and revised paragraph in the answer key on page TK for guidance in answering questions 6 and 7.) Students should recognize that the paragraph is expository because it presents facts about a subject. The first sentence is the topic sentence: *One of the most interesting stories about the beloved American sport of baseball involves a curse.* For question 3, students may point out some of the following facts: The Boston Red Sox won the first World Series in 1903. The Red Sox traded Babe Ruth and other players to the Yankees in 1919. The Red Sox didn't win another World Series after trading Ruth until 2004. Although the concluding sentence is linked to the topic sentence, it doesn't have as much of an impact as it could. As for flow, transition words do help the sentences flow, but they could be smoother.

National Language Arts Standards:

▲ Uses strategies to draft and revise written work

▲ Uses strategies to edit and publish written work

▲ Evaluates own and others' writing

Overhead Transparency

◆ Editing and Proofreading Paragraphs

Reproducibles

◆ Paragraph Checklist

◆ Proofreading Marks

◆ Proofreading Practice, Please!

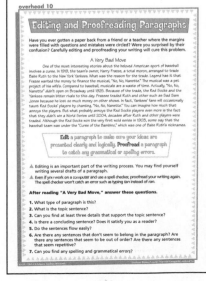

▲ Student Reproducibles

Distribute copies of the reproducibles Paragraph Checklist and Proofreading Marks for students to keep in their notebooks. Store extra copies in the writing center. Have students use the Proofreading Marks reproducible to proof Proofreading Practice, Please!

▲ Writing Practice

Challenge students to revise "A Very Bad Move." Also ask them to use the Paragraph Checklist and Proofreading Marks reproducibles to edit another paragraph they have written. Discuss how using the reproducibles affected their view of the work.

▲ Enriching the Lesson

Asking students to edit and proofread someone else's work can help with their own writing. Emphasize the importance of clearly articulating their questions and concerns. By doing so, students can begin to approach their own work with a clearer eye.

Paragraph Checklist

All Paragraphs:

❑ Is the paragraph indented?

❑ Is the topic sentence clear?

❑ Are there at least three detail sentences in the body of the paragraph to support the topic sentence?

❑ Have I used transition words to help the sentences flow?

❑ Does the paragraph contain any unnecessary words or sentences?

❑ Does the concluding sentence wrap up the paragraph and link to the topic sentence?

Expository Paragraphs:

❑ Does the paragraph present information about a topic?

❑ Have I researched the topic well enough?

❑ Does the paragraph contain at least three facts that support the topic sentence?

❑ Are the facts presented in a logical order?

Descriptive Paragraphs:

❑ Does the paragraph paint a clear picture of a person, place, or thing?

❑ Have I used expressive language?

❑ Have I included sensory details that will help the reader picture the topic?

Narrative Paragraphs:

❑ Does the paragraph tell a story or relate an experience?

❑ Does the paragraph make an important point?

❑ Is the material presented in sequence?

Persuasive Paragraphs:

❑ Does the paragraph begin with a statement that I want to prove?

❑ Have I researched the statement well enough?

❑ Does the paragraph contain at least three facts that support the statement?

❑ Have I used only facts, not opinions, to prove my point?

Grammar, Spelling, Capitalization, and Punctuation:

❑ Have I checked the grammar?

❑ Are all the words in the paragraph spelled correctly?

❑ Have I capitalized all proper nouns?

❑ Is the paragraph punctuated correctly?

Proofreading Marks

Instruction	Proofreader's Mark	Correction
delete	the ~~cold and~~ freezing ice	the freezing ice
delete and close up space	the free͡zing ice	the freezing ice
insert word(s)	last winter ⌄ *in Maine*	last winter in Maine
let it stand	our ~~summer~~ vacation	our summer vacation
spell out	⑨ bluebirds ⓢⓟ	nine bluebirds
new paragraph	"I did." ⌐ "You did not." ¶	"I did." "You did not."
transpose	my friend best ⓣⓡ	my best friend
insert space	Ring⏐the doorbell.	Ring the doorbell
close up space	Who ͡ is it?	Who is it?
insert period	I am so tired ⌄⊙	I am so tired
insert comma	coats⌄shoes⌄and pants	coats, shoes, and pants
insert quotation marks	Read the poem, ⌄Sand.⌄	Read the poem, "Sand."
insert parentheses	Read "Sand" ⌄pages 10–12⌄	Read "Sand" (pages 10–12).
uppercase	thanksgiving day ⓒⓐⓟ	Thanksgiving Day
lowercase	My Birthday ⓛⓒ	my birthday

Proofreading Practice, Please!

**Snow White needs some proofreading help. Her letter contains 10 errors.
Mark the errors using proofreading marks.**

Dear Dwarfs,

    You're probably wondering why I left? I have to admit
I have gotten tired of of you're strange habits. Its no fun
being with people who are sneezing, sleeping, and acting
grumpy all day. Also, it turned out that the prince wasn't
the won for me. I don't want to sit around the castle all day
while he's off slaying dragons. It's so boring.

    The other day, I took a good lok in the mirror. Sure it
said, "You're the fairest of them all." But it also said, "Plan
for the future. Think about your education. Think about
yourcareer." That was it. "Snow, I said, "its time to leave
here. It's time to say good-bye to the dwarfs. I'm going back
two school."

    I hope I haven't hurt your feelings. I appreciate how
generous you've been, but I want to make it on own.

    Your friend,

    Snow White

Answer Key

Page 9: What Am I?

1. expository
2. descriptive
3. narrative
4. persuasive

Page 10: Order! Order!

Possible answer:

    With its hump and long legs, the camel may look funny, but it's uniquely suited to living in the desert. Many people think that a camel's hump is filled with water, but this isn't true. The hump is a mound of fatty tissue that can shrink. If no food is available, a camel gets energy from this fatty tissue. A camel's legs are long and thin, but they are very muscular. These muscles enable the animal to carry heavy loads for long distances.

    For instance, a camel can carry almost 1,000 pounds, but a load of about 400 pounds is the best weight. A walking camel travels about 3 miles per hour. The typical distance a camel can travel in a day is 25 miles. At a gallop, racing camels can do 12 miles per hour.

    When a camel walks, the pads of its feet spread. This keeps the camel's feet from sinking into the sand. The lack of food in a desert and its soft, sandy surface are no problems for a camel!

Page 17: Getting Off to a Good Start

"Quick, Easy, and Cheap Stickers" is the more powerful paragraph because its topic sentence helps the writer focus on clearly presenting the steps in this how-to paragraph.

Page 20: Building a Paragraph (Sample answer is given.)

    Several American cities bill themselves as the "Watermelon Capital"—and they have the watermelons to prove it. For instance, the water tower in Hope, Arkansas, is in the shape of a watermelon. Hope has produced watermelons that weigh more than 100 pounds. Green River, Utah, sports a giant watermelon statue that is 25 feet long. This Utah watermelon statue even has a motor, but it's broken, so the statue doesn't move anymore. Another town with a watermelon-shaped water tower is Luling, Texas. Every summer, Luling hosts the Watermelon Thump. The Watermelon Thump features a car rally and a watermelon-seed-spitting contest. Although about 15 million watermelons are harvested in Dilley, Texas, each year, their watermelon statue is only 5 feet long. The slogan of Dilley is "Self-Proclaimed Watermelon Capital of Texas." There may not be one "Watermelon Capital," but many towns enjoy celebrating this sweet and juicy fruit.

Page 25: Lost in Transition (Sample answer is given.)

Lost in the Wild

Have you ever thought about what might happen if you got lost in the desert, mountains, or forest? If you follow these tips, the chances are good that you'll be rescued quickly. First of all, always tell someone where you are going and what time you expect to return. Next, make sure you're prepared for your trip into the wild by taking along important supplies and equipment. Carry a map and a compass—and make sure you know how to use them. Along with these pieces of equipment, carry a backpack filled with a first-aid kit, extra food and clothing, sunglasses, and a flashlight. Also, wear a whistle around your neck. If you get lost, then blow it three times. Furthermore, you may have to start a fire, so you'll need matches (waterproof) or a lighter. Finally, if you think you're lost, don't keep walking. This might make it more difficult for rescuers to find you. Stay calm. Don't panic because that could cause you to become confused. To repeat, wait for help. While you wait, eat a meal or set up your tent. Remember to keep this in mind: People will be looking for you. If you plan ahead, getting lost will not be a problem.

Page 40: Facts and More Facts (Sample paragraph is given.)

A Day for a Champ

Native Texan Lance Armstrong deserves a state holiday. Born in Plano, Texas, Armstrong now lives in Austin, Texas. Armstrong is the only person to have won six consecutive Tour de France bicycle races in a row. And he achieved this feat after battling cancer. Texas celebrates other heroes, including Cesar Chavez and Lyndon Baines Johnson, with state holidays. On these holidays, state offices have the option of closing or remaining open with a reduced staff. Give Texans the opportunity to celebrate one of the state's great champions and heroes by having a Lance Armstrong state holiday.

Overhead 10: Editing and Proofreading Paragraphs

A Very Bad Move

One of the most interesting stories about the beloved sport of *American* baseball involves a curse. In 1919, the team's *Red Sox* owner, Harry Frazee, ~~a total moron~~, arranged to trade Babe Ruth to the New York Yankees. What was the reason for the trade? Legend has it that Frazee wanted the money to finance the musical, "No, No, Nanette." The musical was a pet project of his wife's. ~~Compared to baseball, musicals are a waste of time.~~ Actually, "No, No, Nanette" didn't open on Broadway until 1925. Because of the trade, the Red Sox and the Yankees remain bitter rivals to this day. Frazee traded Ruth and other players such as Sad Sam Jones because he lost so much money on other shows. In fact, Yankees' fans will occasionally taunt Red Sox players by chanting, "No, No, Nanette." You can imagine how much that annoys the players. But what probably annoys the Red Sox players even more is the fact that they didn't win a World Series until 2004, decades after ~~since~~ Ruth and other players were traded. ~~Although the Red Socks won the very first wold series in 1903,~~ some say that the baseball team was under the "Curse of the Bambino," which was one of Babe Ruth's nicknames.

Page 42: Writing Practice (Sample revision given.)

A Very Bad Move

One of the most interesting stories about the beloved American sport of baseball involves a curse. In 1919, the owner of the Boston Red Sox, Harry Frazee, arranged to trade Babe Ruth to the New York Yankees. What was the reason for the trade? Legend has it that Frazee wanted the money to finance the musical "No, No, Nanette," which was a pet project of his wife's. Actually, "No, No, Nanette" didn't open on Broadway until 1925. Frazee traded Ruth and other players such as Sad Sam Jones because he lost so much money on other shows. Because of the trade, the Red Sox and the Yankees remain bitter rivals to this day. In fact, the Yankees' fans will occasionally taunt Red Sox players by chanting, "No, No, Nanette." That may be annoying, but what really annoyed the Red Sox players and fans is the fact that they didn't win a World Series until 2004, decades after Ruth and other players were traded. As a result, some believe that the baseball team suffered from the "Curse of the Bambino," which was one of Babe Ruth's nicknames.

Page 45: Proofreading Practice, Please!

Dear Dwarfs,

You're probably wondering why I left? I have to admit I have gotten tired of ~~of you're~~ *your* strange habits. It's no fun being with people who are sneezing, sleeping, and acting grumpy all day. Also, it turned out that the prince wasn't the ~~won~~ *one* for me. I don't want to sit around the castle all day while he's off slaying dragons. It's so boring.

The other day, I took a good look in the mirror. Sure it said, "You're the fairest of them all." But it also said, "Plan for the future. Think about your education. Think about your career." That was it. "Snow," I said, "it's time to leave here. It's time to say good-bye to the dwarfs. I'm going back ~~two~~ *to* school."

I hope I haven't hurt your feelings. I appreciate how generous you've been, but I want to make it on *my* own.

Your friend,

Snow White